The **ESSENTIALS**® of

Italian

DO726058

Carmela Ciarcia Forte, M.A.
Queens College
Queens, New York

Raymond M. Mantione, M.A.
Italian Instructor
Adult Education
Edison, New Jersey

Research & Education Association
Visit our website at
www.rea.com

Research & Education Association
61 Ethel Road West
Piscataway, New Jersey 08854
E-mail: info@rea.com

THE ESSENTIALS®
OF ITALIAN

Year 2006 Printing

Copyright © 2001, 1999, 1994 by Research & Education Association, Inc. All rights reserved. No part of this book may be reproduced in any form without permission of the publisher.

Printed in the United States of America

Library of Congress Control Number 00-11317

International Standard Book Number 0-87891-929-5

ESSENTIALS® and REA® are registered trademarks of Research & Education Association, Inc.

What REA's Essentials®
Will Do for You

This book is part of REA's celebrated *Essentials*® series of review and study guides, relied on by tens of thousands of students over the years for being complete yet concise.

Here you'll find a summary of the very material you're most likely to need for exams, not to mention homework—eliminating the need to read and review many pages of textbook and class notes.

This slim volume condenses the vast amount of detail characteristic of the subject matter and summarizes the **essentials** of the field. The book provides quick access to the important principles, vocabulary, grammar, and structures in the language.

It will save you hours of study and preparation time.

This *Essentials*® book has been prepared by experts in the field and has been carefully reviewed to ensure its accuracy and maximum usefulness. We believe you'll find it a valuable, handy addition to your library.

Larry B. Kling
Chief Editor

Contents

Chapter 1
PRONOUNCING ITALIAN 1
   1.1   Letters and Pronunciation 1
   1.2   Special Consonant Sounds 1
   1.3   Syllabication and Stress 2
   1.4   Double Consonants 3
   1.5   The Silent H 3

Chapter 2
AUXILIARY VERBS *AVERE* AND *ESSERE* 4
   2.1   *Avere:* Present Tense 4
   2.2   *Avere:* Idiomatic Expressions 4
   2.3   *Essere:* Present Tense 5
   2.4   *Essere:* Idiomatic Expressions 6
   2.5   Past Participles 6
   2.6   Present Perfect 6
   2.7   Present Participle (Gerund) of *Avere* and *Essere* 7
   2.8   Imperfect 7
   2.9   Present Subjunctive 8
   2.10 Imperfect Subjunctive 8
   2.11 Past Subjunctive 9
   2.12 Future 9
   2.13 Present Conditional 10
   2.14 Preterite 10
   2.15 Imperative 11

Chapter 3
CONJUGATIONS OF REGULAR VERBS 12
   3.1   Regular Verbs 12
   3.2   Compound Past Tenses 14
   3.3   Present Gerunds 16
   3.4   Imperfect: Formation and Use 16
   3.5   Present Subjunctive: Formation and Use 17

3.6   Formation of Imperfect Subjunctive Verbs
       –are, –ere, –ire 20
3.7   Past Subjunctive 20
3.8   Future and Conditional: Formation and Use 21
3.9   The Preterite: Formation and Use 23
3.10   Negatives 24
3.11   Imperative 25
3.12   Passive Construction 25
3.13   Causative Construction 25
3.14   Impersonal Expressions 26
3.15   Infinitive Constructions 26
3.16   If/Then Clauses 27
3.17   Reflexive Verbs 27

Chapter 4
CONJUGATIONS OF IRREGULAR VERBS 29
4.1   Common Irregular *–are* Verbs 29
4.2   Common Irregular *–ere* Verbs 31
4.3   Common Irregular *–ire* Verbs 33
4.4   Irregular Past Participles with *Avere* 34
4.5   Irregular Past Participles with *Essere* 36
4.6   Irregular Present Gerunds 36

Chapter 5
NUMBERS AND TIME 37
5.1   Cardinal Numbers 37
5.2   Ordinal Numbers 38
5.3   Expressing Time 39

Chapter 6
DAYS, MONTHS, SEASONS, AND DATES 41
6.1   Days of the Week 41
6.2   Months of the Year 41
6.3   Seasons and Weather 42
6.4   Dates 44

Chapter 7
TOPICAL VOCABULARY

TOPICAL VOCABULARY 45
7.1   Home 45
7.2   Foods 45
7.3   Beverages 46
7.4   Vegetables 46
7.5   Recreation 46
7.6   Sports 46
7.7   Parts of the Body 47
7.8   Colors 47
7.9   Clothing 47
7.10   Jewelry 47
7.11   Occupations 48
7.12   Transportation 48
7.13   Courses 48
7.14   Fruit 49
7.15   Animals 49

Chapter 8
NOUNS AND DEFINITE AND INDEFINITE ARTICLES

NOUNS AND DEFINITE AND INDEFINITE ARTICLES 50
8.1   The Gender of Nouns 50
8.2   Common Exceptions to the Rule 51
8.3   Irregular Plurals 52
8.4   Suffixes 53
8.5   Definite Articles 54
8.6   Definite Article Contractions 55
8.7   Indefinite Articles 55

Chapter 9
REGULAR AND IRREGULAR ADJECTIVES

REGULAR AND IRREGULAR ADJECTIVES 57
9.1   Regular Adjectives 57
9.2   Irregular Adjectives 58
9.3   Shortened Adjectives 59
9.4   Titles 60
9.5   Comparison of Adjectives 60
9.6   Relative Superlative of Adjectives 61
9.7   Absolute Superlative of Adjectives 61
9.8   Irregular Comparatives and Superlatives 61

9.9   Possessive Adjectives 62
9.10 Demonstrative Adjectives 63

Chapter 10
PRONOUNS 65

10.1   Subject Pronouns 65
10.2   Direct Object Pronouns 65
10.3   Indirect Object Pronouns *Mi, Ti, Ci*, and *Vi* 66
10.4   Indirect Object Pronouns *Gli, Le*, and *Loro* 66
10.5   *Ci* 67
10.6   *Ne* 67
10.7   Double Object Pronouns 68
10.8   *Glielo, Gliela, Glieli*, and *Gliele* 68
10.9   *Loro* 69
10.10 Pronouns in Informal Commands 69
10.11 Pronouns in Formal Commands.................. 69
10.12 Disjunctive Pronouns 69

Chapter 11
ADVERBS 71

11.1   Regular Adverbs 71
11.2   Irregular Adverbs 71
11.3   Formation of Adverbs 72
11.4   Position 73
11.5   Irregular Comparatives and Superlatives 73

GLOSSARY 74

CHAPTER 1

Pronouncing Italian

1.1 Letters and Pronunciation

Italian is a very phonetic language, which means that it is spoken the way it is written. Its alphabet consists of 21 letters.

The Alphabet and Its Pronunciation

a = a (ah)	*h = acca (accah)*	*q = cu (coo)*
b = bi (bee)	*i = i (ee)*	*r = erre (erray)*
c = ci (chee)	*l = elle (ellay)*	*s = esse (essay)*
d = di (dee)	*m = emme (emmay)*	*t = ti (tee)*
e = e (eh)	*n = enne (ennay)*	*u = u (ooh)*
f = effe (effay)	*o = o (oh)*	*v = vu (voo)*
g = gi (gee)	*p = pi (pee)*	*z = zeta (tsaytah)*

Letters found in foreign words are:

j = *i lunga (ee lungah)*   **k** = *cappa (cappah)*
w = *doppiovu (doppiovoo)*   **x** = *ics (eeks)*
y = *ipsilon (ipseelone)*

1.2 Special Consonant Sounds

The hard sound of **c** and **g** before **a, o, u:**

ca as in "carpenter"; *casa*   **ga** as "garland"; *gatto*

co as in "colon"; *cosa* **go** as in "gopher"; *gola*
cu as in "cuckoo"; *curioso* **gu** as in "guru"; *gusto*

The soft sound of **c** and **g** before **e, i**:

ce as in "cherry"; *celeste* **ge** as in "gender"; *gelato*
ci as in "cheek"; *cinema* **gi** as in "gene"; *giorno*

The sound of **ci, ce** and **gi, ge** changes to a hard sound when an **h** follows the **c** or **g**:

chi as in "key"; *chiaro, chiesa* **ghi** as in "geese"; *ghiaccio*
che as in "Kay"; *perchè, Michele* **ghe** as in "gay"; *larghe*

gli is an unusual sound not found in English pronunciation. The closest sound to it is the double l of "million"; *figli, foglio*

gn sounds like "on" as in "onion"; *signore, sogno*

r is produced by gently fluttering the tongue against the roof of the mouth; *rosso, rosa, glorioso.*

z has a **ts** sound in *grazie, zucchero* and a **dz** sound in *zero, mezzo.*

sc before an **i** or an **e** has the sound of the English word "she." For example, *lo sci; sciare; capisce.*

sc followed by an **h** has the sound of the English word "ski." For example, *schiavo; scheletro; schema.*

1.3 Syllabication and Stress

These consonant clusters, **ch, gh, gl, gn,** and **sc,** count as single consonants.

A single consonant between two vowels belongs to the following syllable; *ca-sa, la-ghi, lar-ghe.*

When **l** or **r** follows a second consonant and occurs between vowels, the consonant group belongs to the following syllable; *qua-dro, nu-cle-are.*

When a double consonant occurs between two vowels or between **l** or **r**, the first consonant belongs to the preceding syllable, the second to the following syllables; *mam-ma, sor-el-la.*

1.3.1 Stress

Most Italian words stress the next-to-last syllable:

*finestra (fi-**ne**-stra)*
*lavagna (la-**va**-gna)*

If a word is stressed on the last syllable it must be accented:

*caffè (caf-**fè**)*
*bontà (bon-**tà**)*

Note: When stress is not shown as part of the spelling, it is difficult to determine which syllable is stressed:

*gondola (**gon**-do-la)*
*camera (**ca**-me-ra)*

1.4 Double Consonants

A single consonant is pronounced with a concise, clipped, sharp sound, whereas a double consonant is held for two beats as in music; *sete/sette, rosa/rossa, papa/pappa.*

1.5 The Silent H

The letter **h** has no sound of its own, but it changes the pronunciation of other letters:
io ho
tu hai
egli ha

CHAPTER 2

Auxiliary Verbs *Avere* and *Essere*

2.1 *Avere:* Present Tense

The verb *avere* (to have) is an irregular verb. Its forms in the present tense are:

Singular	Plural
io ho – I have	*noi abbiamo* – we have
tu hai – you have (familiar)	*voi avete* – you have (familiar)
lei/ella ha – she, it has	*loro hanno* – they have
lui/egli ha – he, it has	*essi/esse hanno* – they have
Lei ha – you have (formal)	*Loro hanno* – you have (formal)

2.2 *Avere:* Idiomatic Expressions

Many idioms are formed with *avere*. The most common of these are:

avere caldo – to be hot
Gianni ha caldo in estate. Johnny is hot in summer.

avere freddo – to be cold
Noi abbiamo freddo in inverno. We are cold in winter.

avere fame – to be hungry
Lui ha fame a mezzogiorno. He's hungry at noon.

avere sete – to be thirsty
Io ho sete quando fa caldo. I'm thirsty when it's hot.

avere sonno – to be sleepy
Gli alunni hanno sonno nella classe. The students are sleepy in
    class.

avere paura – to be afraid
Maria ha paura del lupo. Mary is afraid of the wolf.

avere fretta – to be in a hurry
Il professore ha fretta. The teacher is in a hurry.

avere ragione – to be right
Il babbo ha sempre ragione. Dad is always right.

avere torto – to be wrong
La mamma non ha mai torto. Mom is never wrong.

avere...anni – to be...years old
Quanti anni hai? How old are you?
Ho ventun anni. I'm 21 years old.

2.3 *Essere:* Present Tense

The verb *essere* (to be) is an irregular verb. Its forms in the present
tense are:

Singular	Plural
io sono – I am	*noi siamo* – we are
tu sei – you are (familiar)	*voi siete* – you are (familiar)

lei/ella è – she, it is
lui/egli è – he, it is
Lei è – you are (formal)

loro sono – they are
essi/esse sono – they are
Loro sono – you are (formal)

Note: Both the *io* and *loro* forms use *sono.*

2.4 *Essere:* Idiomatic Expressions

essere di – to be from
Di dove sei? Sono di Roma. Where are you from? I'm from Rome.

essere di – to belong to
Di chi è la penna? È di Rosa. Whose pen is it? It's Rosa's.

c'è/ci sono – there is/there are
C'è uno sbaglio. There is a mistake. *Ci sono sbagli.* There are
mistakes.

com'è/come sono? – how is, how are? (used to elicit descrip-
tions)
Com'è Angelina? È una ragazza simpatica. How is Angelina?
[describe her] She's a lovely girl.
Come sono la pasta? E deliziosa. How's the pasta? It's delicious.

2.5 Past Participles

Avere = avuto (had)
Essere = stato/a/i/e (been)

2.6 Present Perfect

Avere

Singular	Plural
io ho avuto – I had	*noi abbiamo avuto*
tu hai avuto	*voi avete avuto*
lei/ella ha avuto	*loro hanno avuto*
lui/egli ha avuto	*essi/esse hanno avuto*
Lei ha avuto	*Loro hanno avuto*

Essere

Singular	Plural
io sono stato(a) – I have been	*noi siamo stati(e)* – we were
tu sei stato(a)	*voi siete stati(e)*
lei/ella è stato(a)	*loro sono stati(e)*
lui/egli è stato(a)	*essi/esse sono stati(e)*
Lei è stato(a)	*Loro sono stati(e)*

2.7 Present Participle (Gerund) of *Avere* and *Essere*

Avere = avendo – having
Essere = essendo – being

2.8 Imperfect

Avere

Singular	Plural
io avevo – I used to have	*noi avevamo*
tu avevi	*voi avevate*
lei/ella aveva	*loro avevano*
lui/egli aveva	*essi/esse avevano*
Lei aveva	*Loro avevano*

Essere

Singular	Plural
io ero – I used to be	*noi eravamo*
tu eri	*voi eravate*
lei/ella era	*loro erano*
lui/egli era	*essi/esse erano*
Lei era	*Loro erano*

2.9 Present Subjunctive

Avere

Singular	Plural
che io abbia – that I may have	*che noi abbiamo*
che tu abbia	*che voi abbiate*
che lei/ella abbia	*che loro abbiano*
che lui/egli abbia	*che essi/esse abbiano*
che Lei abbia	*che Loro abbiano*

Essere

Singular	Plural
che io sia – that I may be	*che noi siamo*
che tu sia	*che voi siate*
che lei/ella sia	*che loro siano*
che lui/egli sia	*che essi/esse siano*
che Lei sia	*che Loro siano*

2.10 Imperfect Subjunctive

Avere

Singular	Plural
che io avessi – that I might have	*che noi avessimo*
che tu avessi	*che voi aveste*
che lei/ella avesse	*che loro avessero*
che lui/egli avesse	*che essi/esse avessero*
che Lei avesse	*che Loro avessero*

Essere

Singular	Plural
che io fossi – that I might be	*che noi fossimo*
che tu fossi	*che voi foste*
che lei/ella fosse	*che loro fossero*
che lui/egli fosse	*che essi/esse fossero*
che Lei fosse	*che Loro fossero*

2.11 Past Subjunctive

Avere

Singular	Plural
che io abbia avuto – that I may have had	*che noi abbiamo avuto*
che tu abbia avuto	*che voi abbiate avuto*
che lei/ella abbia avuto	*che loro abbiano avuto*
che lui/egli abbia avuto	*che essi/esse abbiano avuto*
che Lei abbia avuto	*che Loro abbiano avuto*

Essere

Singular	Plural
che io sia stato(a) – that I may have been	*che noi siamo stati(e)*
che tu sia stato(a)	*che voi siate stati(e)*
che lei/ella sia stato	*che loro siano stati(e)*
che lui/egli sia stato	*che essi/esse siano stati(s)tate*
che Lei sia stato	*che Loro siano stati(e)*

2.12 Future

Avere

Singular	Plural
io avrò – I shall have	*noi avremo*
tu avrai	*voi avrete*
lei/ella avrà	*loro avranno*
lui/egli avrà	*essi/esse avranno*
Lei avrà	*Loro avranno*

Essere

Singular	Plural
io sarò – I shall be	*noi saremo*
tu sarai	*voi sarete*
lei/ella sarà	*loro saranno*

lui/egli sarà   essi/esse sarano
Lei sarà   Loro sarano

2.13 Present Conditional

Avere

Singular	Plural
io avrei – I should have	*noi avremmo*
tu avresti	*voi avreste*
lei/ella avrebbe	*loro avrebbero*
lui/egli avrebbe	*essi/esse avrebbero*
Lei avrebbe	*Loro avrebbero*

Essere

Singular	Plural
io sarei – I should be	*noi saremmo*
tu saresti	*voi sareste*
lei/ella sarebbe	*loro sarebbero*
lui/egli sarebbe	*essi/esse sarebbero*
Lei sarebbe	*Loro sarebbero*

2.14 Preterite

Avere

Singular	Plural
io ebbi – I had	*noi avemmo*
tu avesti	*voi aveste*
lei/ella ebbe	*loro ebbero*
lui/egli ebbe	*essi/esse ebbero*
Lei ebbe	*Loro ebbero*

Essere

Singular – Plural	
io fui – I was	*noi fummo*
tu fosti	*voi foste*
lei/ella fu	*loro furono*

lui/egli fu   *essi/esse furono*
Lei fu   *Loro furono*

2.15 Imperative

Avere

Singular	Plural
tu abbi – have	*noi abbiamo* – let's have
Lei abbia	*voi abbiate*
	Loro abbiano

Essere

Singular	Plural
tu sii – be	*noi siamo* – let's be
Lei sia	*voi siate*
	Loro siano

CHAPTER 3

Conjugations of Regular Verbs

3.1 Regular Verbs

Regular verbs are divided into three conjugations according to their endings: *–are, –ere,* and *–ire.*

3.1.1 Present Indicative (*–are* Verbs)

Parlare (to speak)

Singular	Plural
io parlo – I speak	*noi parliamo* – we speak
tu parli – you speak (familiar)	*voi parlate* – you speak (familiar)
lei/ella parla – she speaks	*loro parlano* – you speak
lui/egli parla – he speaks	*essi/esse parlano* – they speak
Lei parla – you speak (formal)	*Loro parlano* – you speak (formal)

3.1.2 Present Indicative (*–ere* Verbs)

Scrivere (to write)

Singular	Plural
io scrivo – I write	*noi scriviamo* – we write
tu scrivi – you write	*voi scrivete* – you write (familiar)

lei/ella scrive – she writes (familiar)

lui/egli scrive – he writes

Lei scrive – you write (formal)

loro scrivono – you write

essi/esse scrivono – you write

Loro scrivono – you write (formal)

There are two groups of *–ire* verbs: non-*isc* verbs and *–isc* verbs. Non-*isc* verbs are recognized by two or more consonants before the *–ire* ending.

3.1.3 Present Indicative (*–ire*, non-*isc* Verbs):

Partire

Singular	Plural
io parto – I leave	*noi partiamo* – we leave
tu parti – you leave (familiar)	*voi partite* – you leave (familiar)
lei/ella parte – she leaves	*loro partono* – they leave
lui/egli parte – he leaves	*essi/esse partono* – they leave
Lei parte – you leave (formal)	*Loro partono* – you leave (formal)

3.1.4 Present Indicative (*–ire*, *–isc* Verbs):

–isc verbs usually have one consonant before the *–ire* ending.

Capire

Singular	Plural
io capisco – I understand	*noi capiamo* – we understand
tu capisci – you understand (familiar)	*voi capite* – you understand (familiar)
lei/ella capisce – she understands	*loro capiscono* – they understand
lui/egli capisce – he understands	*essi/esse capiscono* – they understand
Lei capisce – you understand (formal)	*Loro capiscono* – you understand (formal)

3.2 Compound Past Tenses

The compound past tense is formed by the present tense of *avere* or *essere* plus the past participle.

The past participle of regular verbs is formed as follows:

Verb	Ending	Past Participle
parlare – are – ato		*parlato* – spoke
vendere – ere – uto		*venduto* – sold
dormire – ire – ito		*dormito* – slept

3.2.1 Present Perfect with *Avere*

The following verbs use *avere* as an auxiliary verb:

Parlare

Singular	Plural
io ho parlato – I spoke, I have spoken, I did speak	*noi abbiamo parlato*
tu hai parlato	*voi avete parlato*
lei/ella ha parlato	*essi/esse hanno parlato*
lui/egli ha parlato	
Lei ha parlato	*Loro hanno parlato*

Vendere

Singular	Plural
io ho venduto – I sold, I have sold, I did sell	*noi abbiamo venduto*
tu hai venduto	*voi avete venduto*
lei/ella ha venduto	*essi/esse hanno venduto*
lui/egli ha venduto	
Lei ha venduto	*Loro hanno venduto*

Dormire

Singular	Plural
io ho dormito – I slept, I have slept, I did sleep	*noi abbiamo dormito*
tu hai dormito	*voi avete dormito*
lei/ella ha dormito	*essi/esse hanno dormito*
lui/egli ha dormito	
Lei ha dormito	*Loro hanno dormito*

3.2.2 Present Perfect with *Essere*

Verbs of motion (for example, coming and going) use *essere* as an auxiliary verb. When conjugating with *essere*, the past participle must agree with the subject in gender and number. Reflexive verbs also follow the same rule.

Andare

Singular	Plural
io sono andato(a) – I did go, I have gone, I went	*noi siamo andati(e)*
tu sei andato(a)	*voi siete andati(e)*
lei/ella è andata	*essi/esse sono andati(e)*
lui/egliè andato(a)	
Lei è andato(a)	*Loro sono andati(e)*

3.2.3 Regular Verbs Using *Essere*

The following verbs have a regular past participle and use *essere:*

andare – to go
arrivare – to arrive
cadere – to fall
diventare – to become
entrare – to enter
partire – to depart

ritornare – to return, to come back
salire – to go up
scappare – to run away
stare – to stay
tornare – to return, to come back
uscire – to go out

3.3 Present Gerunds

The gerunds of regular verbs are formed as follows:

Ending	Verb	Present Participle	
–are ⇒ *ando*	*parlare*	*parlando*	speaking
–ere ⇒ *endo*	*vendere*	*vendendo*	selling
–ire ⇒ *endo*	*dormire*	*dormendo*	sleeping

3.3.1 Present Progressive

To form the present progressive, use the present tense of *stare* plus the present gerund.

Parlare

Singular	Plural
io sto parlando – I am speaking	*noi stiamo parlando*
tu stai parlando	*voi state parlando*
lei/ella sta parlando	*essi/esse stanno parlando*
lui/eglista parlando	
Lei sta parlando	*Loro stanno parlando*

3.4 Imperfect: Formation and Use

Parlare

Singular	Plural
io parlavo – I was speaking, I used to speak	*noi parlavamo*
tu parlavi	*voi parlavate*
lei/ella parlava	*essi/esse parlavano*
lui/egli parlava	
Lei parlava	*Loro parlavano*

Scrivere

Singular	Plural
io scrivevo – I used to write, I was writing	*noi scrivevamo*

16

Singular	Plural
tu scrivevi	voi scrivevate
lei/ella scriveva	essi/esse scrivevano
lui/egli scriveva	
Lei scriveva	Loro scrivevano

Partire

Singular	Plural
io partivo – I was leaving, I used to leave	noi partivamo
tu partivi	voi partivate
lui/egli partiva	essi/esse partivano
lei/ella partiva	
Lei partiva	Loro partivano

The imperfect tense indicates continuous action in the past and is translated as "was," "were," and "used to."

> *Quando ero piccolo, parlavo sempre con il nonno.* When I was young, I always used to talk with grandpa.

3.5 Present Subjunctive: Formation and Use

Parlare

Singular	Plural
che io parli – that I may speak	che noi parliamo
che tu parli	che voi parliate
che lei/ella parli	che essi/esse parlino
che lui/egli parli	
che Lei parli	che Loro parlino

Scrivere

Singular	Plural
che io scriva – that I may write	che noi scriviamo
che tu scriva	che voi scriviate
che lei/ella scriva	che essi/esse scrivano

che lui/egli scriva
che Lei scriva   *che Loro scrivano*

Partire

Singular	Plural
che io parta – that I may leave	*che noi partiamo*
che tu parta	*che voi partiate*
che lei/ella parta	*che essi/esse partano*
che lui/egli parta	
che Lei parta	*che Loro partano*

The subjunctive mood conveys the speaker's emotion or attitude—for example, uncertainty, possibility, doubt, or anger.

È probabile che gli studenti scrivano tutti gli esercizi. It is likely that the students will do all the exercises.

The subjunctive is used if there is a chance that the action has not taken place or may not take place.

Non credo che siano partiti per Roma. I don't believe they departed for Rome.

Some common verbs that require the subjunctive are:

arrabbiarsi – to become angry
comandare – to command, to order
desiderare – to wish
esigere – to demand

essere sorpreso – to be surprised
insistere – to insist
negare – to deny

permettere – to permit, to allow
pretendere – to demand

avere paura – to be afraid
consentire – to allow, to permit
dispiacersi – to be sorry
essere contento – to be happy
essere triste – to be sad
lasciare – to let
ordinare – to order, to command
preferire – to prefer
proibire – to forbid

18

richiedere – to require, to demand
suggerire – to suggest
volere – to want

sperare – to hope
temere – to fear

Subjunctive with impersonal expressions:

è necessario che... – it is necessary that...
è impossibile che... – it is impossible that...
è probabile che... – it is probable that...
si dubita che... – it is doubtful that...

Si dubita che il Presidente Clinton lo sappia. It is doubtful that President Clinton knows it.

Subjunctive with subordinate conjunctions:

prima che – before
senza che – without
purchè – provided that
a meno che – non, unless
poichè – since
dovunque – wherever
quantunque – although

opo che – after
non appena che – as soon as
in modo che – so that
sebbene – although
chiunque – whoever
qualunque – whatever

Prima che Luigi parta voglio vederlo. Before Louis leaves, I want to see him.

Subjunctive verbs ending in *–care* and *–gare* add *h* before subjunctive endings.

toccare – to touch   *che io tocchi*

Verbs ending in *–ciare* and in *–giare* drop *–iare* before adding subjunctive endings.

cominciare – to begin   *che io cominci*

19

3.6 Formation of Imperfect Subjunctive Verbs –*are*, –*ere*, –*ire*

Parlare

Singular	Plural
che io parlassi – that I might speak	*che noi parlassimo*
che tu parlassi	*che voi parlaste*
che lei/ella parlasse	*che essi/esse parlassero*
che lui/egli parlasse	
che Lei parlasse	*che Loro parlassero*

Scrivere

Singular	Plural
che io scrivessi – that I might write	*che noi scrivessimo*
che tu scrivessi	*che voi scriveste*
che lei/ella scrivesse	*che essi/esse scrivessero*
che lui/egli scrivesse	
che Lei scrivesse	*che Loro scrivessero*

Capire

Singular	Plural
che io capissi – that I might understand	*che noi capissimo*
che tu capissi	*che voi capiste*
che lei/ella capisse	*che essi/esse capissero*
che lui/egli capisse	
che Lei capisse	*che Loro capissero*

3.7 Past Subjunctive

To form the past subjunctive, use the present subjunctive of *avere* or *essere* and the past participle.

Parlare

Singular	Plural
che io abbia parlato – that I spoke	*che noi abbiamo parlato*
che tu abbia parlato	*che voi abbiate parlato*
che lei/ella abbia parlato	*che essi/esse abbiano parlato*
che lui/egli abbia parlato	
che Lei abbia parlato	*che Loro abbiano parlato*

Partire

Singular	Plural
che io sia partito(a) – I departed	*che noi siamo partiti(e)*
che tu sia partito(a)	*che voi siate partiti(e)*
che lei/ella sia partita	*che essi siano partiti*
che lui/egli sia partito	*che essi/esse siano partite*
che Lei sia partito(a)	*che Loro siano partiti(e)*

3.8 Future and Conditional: Formation and Use

To form the future and the conditional tenses in verbs, drop *–are* and add *–er* to the stem. For *–ere* and *–ire* verbs, drop the final *e*. The future endings are: *–ò, –i, –à, –emo, –ete, –anno.*

Parlare

Singular	Plural
io parlerò – I shall speak	*noi parleremo*
tu parlerai	*voi parlerete*
lei/ella parlerà	*essi/esse parleranno*
lui/egli parlerà	
Lei parlerà	*Loro parleranno*

Scrivere

Singular	Plural
io scriverò – I shall write	*noi scriveremo*
tu scriverai	*voi scriverete*

21

lei/ella scriverà	*essi/esse scriveranno*
lui/egli scriverà	
Lei scriverà	*Loro scriveranno*

Finire

Singular	Plural
io finirò – I shall finish	*noi finiremo*
tu finirai	*voi finirete*
lei/ella finirà	*essi/esse finiranno*
lui/egli finirà	
Lei finirà	*Loro finiranno*

The conditional endings are: *–ei, –esti, –ebbe, –emmo, –este, –ebbero.*

Parlare

Singular	Plural
io parlerei – I should speak	*noi parleremmo*
tu parleresti	*voi parlereste*
lei/ella parlerebbe	*essi/esse parlerebbero*
lui/egli parlerebbe	
Lei parlerebbe	*Loro parlerebbero*

Scrivere

Singular	Plural
io scriverei – I should write	*noi scriveremmo*
tu scriveresti	*voi scrivereste*
lei/ella scriverebbe	*essi/esse scriverebbero*
lui/egli scriverebbe	
Lei scriverebbe	*Loro scriverebbero*

Finire

Singular	Plural
io finirei – I should finish	*noi finiremmo*
tu finiresti	*voi finireste*

lei/ella finirebbe	*essi/esse finirebbero*
lui/egli finirebbe	
Lei finirebbe	*Loro finirebbero*

The future is translated as "shall" in the first person singular or plural ("I shall," "we shall") and as "will" elsewhere.

Domani finirò il mio lavoro. Tomorrow I shall finish my work.

The conditional is translated as "should" in the first person singular or plural ("I should," "we should") and as "will" elsewhere.

Io gli scriverei se lui venirebbe. I would write to him if he would come.

3.9 The Preterite: Formation and Use

The preterite of regular *–are* verbs is formed by dropping the verb ending and adding: *–ai, –asti, –ò, –ammo, –aste, –arono.*

Parlare

Singular	Plural
io parlai – I spoke	*noi parlammo*
tu parlasti	*voi parlaste*
lei/ella parlò	*essi/esse parlarono*
lui/egli parlò	
Lei parlò	*Loro parlarono*

For *–ere* verbs drop *–ere* and add: *–ei, –esti, –è, –emmo, –este,* and *–erono.*

Scrivere

Singular	Plural
io scrivei – I wrote	*noi scrivemmo*
tu scrivesti	*voi scriveste*
lei/ella scrivè	*essi/esse scriverono*

lui/egli scrivè
Lei scrivè   *Loro scriverono*

Capire	
Singular	**Plural**
io capii – I understood	*noi capimmo*
tu capisti	*voi capiste*
lei/ella capì	*essi/esse capirono*
lui/egli capì	
Lei capì	*Loro capirono*

The preterite is historical tense used in literature to express an action in the past that has no relation to the present.

3.10 Negatives

non – not
non...ancora – not...yet
non...mai – never, not...even
non...che – only
non...niente (nulla) – nothing, not...anything
non...nè...nè – neither...nor, not...either...or
non...nessuno – nobody, no one
non...affatto – not...at all
not – anybody, not...anyone
non...neanche (nemmeno, neppure) – not even
non...più – no longer, not...any more

Place *non* before a verb to make negative. When using a compound negative, place *non* before the verb and the second part of the negative after the verb.

La mamma non sta bene. Mom doesn't feel well.
Questo libro non è più usato. This book is no longer used.

Note: Put *mai* before the past participle in a compound tense.

Non ho mai visitato Parigi. I have never visited Paris.

24

3.11 Imperative

The following forms are used in commands:

	tu	Lei	voi	vui	Loro
are	parla	parli	parlate	parliamo	parlino
ere	scrivi	scriva	scrivete	scriviamo	scrivano
ire	parti	parta	partite	partiamo	partano
ire(isco)	finisci	finisca	finite	finiamo	finiscano

Note: In the negative, use the infinitive of all verbs to form the imperative *tu*.

Non mangiare così. Don't eat like that!

3.12 Passive Construction

To form the passive voice, use the reflexive pronoun *si* with the third person singular or plural of the verb.

Qui si parla italiano. Italian is spoken here.
Si vendono vestiti qui. Suits are sold here.

3.13 Causative Construction

Use *fare* followed by the infinitive to express having something done or made.

Il maestro fa studiare gli alunni. The teacher makes the students study.

Il professore fa studiare la lezione agli studenti. The professor has the students study the lesson.

If there are two objects in a causative sentence, the person become, an indirect object and is introduced by the preposition *â*.

3.14 Impersonal Expressions

Use indirect object pronouns with the following impersonal expressions. Note that the subject follows the verb.

bastare – to be enough
Gli basta un pò di tempo. He needs a little time.

dolere or fare male – to hurt, to be painful
Le fa male la testa. You have a headache.

sembrare – to appear
Loro sembrano strani! They seem strange!

piacere – to like, to be pleasing
Le piace la musica classica. You like classical music.

occorrere – to be necessary
Agli sposi occorrono molti soldi. The newlyweds need lots of money.

3.15 Infinitive Constructions

Use the infinitive after the prepositions *per, prima di, senza.*

Prima di andare a scuola, ho mangiato una pizza. Before going to school, I ate pizza.

Use the past infinitive after *dopo.*

Dopo aver studiato, ho celebrato. After having studied, I celebrated.

The infinitive can be used as a noun.

Mangiare troppo non è buono. Eating too much is not good.

The infinitive is used to give a command.

Scrivere! – Write!
Leggere! – Read!
Studiare! – Study!

3.16 If/Then Clauses

Se (if) clauses express contrary-to-fact conditions. Verb tenses are combined as follows:

Tense Used in the Main Clause	Tense Used in the *Se* Clause
Future	Present Indicative
Conditional Imperfect	Subjunctive
Conditional Perfect	Pluperfect Subjunctive

Note: The present subjunctive is never used after *se*.

Andrai in Francia se hai i soldi. You will go to France if you have the money.

Andresti in Francia se avessi i soldi. You would go to France if you had the money.

Saresti andato in Francia se avessi avuto i soldi. You would have gone to France if you had had the money.

3.17 Reflexive Verbs

The reflexive pronouns precede the verb except in infinitive and informal commands.

Lavarsi

Present: Singular	Plural
io mi lavo – I wash myself	*noi ci laviamo*
tu ti lavi	*voi vi lavate*
lei/ella si lava	*loro si lavano*
lui/egli si lava	*essi/esse si lavano*
Lei si lava	*Loro si lavano*

27

Imperative: informal **formal**
lavati *Si lavi*
lavatevi *Si lavino*
laviamoci

The meaning of a verb changes when it is used reflexively, for example:

alzare – to rise *alzarsi* – to get up
chiamare – to call *chiamarsi* – to be named
divertire – to enjoy *divertirsi* – to amuse oneself

CHAPTER 4

Conjugations of Irregular Verbs

4.1   Common Irregular –*are* Verbs

andare – to go
dare – to give
fare – to do; to make
stare – to stay; to be with health and location

andare – to go

Gerund – *andando*
Past Participle – *andato va*
Present – *vado, vai, va, andiamo, andate, vanno*
Present Subjunctive – *vada, vada, vada, andiamo, andiate, vadano*
Future – *andrò, andrai, andrà, andremo, andrete, andranno*
Conditional – *andrei, andresti, andrebbe, andremmo, andreste, andrebbero*
Imperative – *và (vai), vada, andiamo, andate, adano*

dare – to give

Gerund – *dando*
Past Participle – *dato*
Present – *do, dai, dà, diamo, date, danno*
Present Subjunctive – *dia, dia, dia, diamo, diate, diano*
Imperfect Subjunctive – *dessi, dessi, desse, dessimo, deste, dessero*
Preterite – *diedi, desti, diede, demmo, deste, diedero (dettero)*
Future – *darò, darai, darà, daremo, darete, daranno*
Conditional – *darei, daresti, darebbe, daremmo, dareste, darebbero*
Imperative – *dà (dai), dia, diamo, date, diano*

fare – to do, to make

Gerund – *facendo*
Past Participle – *fatto*
Present – *faccio, fai, fa, facciamo, fate, fanno*
Present Subjunctive – *faccia, faccia, faccia, facciamo, facciate, facciano*
Imperfect – *facevo, facevi, faceva, facevamo, facevate, facevano*
Imperfect Subjunctive – *facessi, facessi, facesse, facessimo, faceste, facessero*
Preterite – *feci, facesti, fece, facemmo, faceste, fecero*
Future – *farò, farai, farà, faremo, farete, faranno*
Conditional – *farei, faresti, farebbe, faremmo, fareste, farebbero*
Imperative – *fà, (fai), faccia, facciamo, fate, facciano*

stare – to stay, to be

Gerund – *stando*
Past Participle – *stato*
Present – *sto, stai, sta, stiamo, state, stanno*
Present Subjunctive – *stia, stia, stia, stiamo, stiate, stiano*
Imperfect – *stiamo, state*
Imperfect Subjunctive – *stessi, stessi, stesse, stessimo, steste, stessero*
Preterite – *stetti, stesti, stette, stemmo, steste, stettero*

Future – *starò, starai, starà, staremo, starete, staranno*
Conditional – *starei, staresti, starebbe, staremmo, stareste, starebbero*
Imperative – *stà (stai), stia, stiano*

4.2 Common Irregular –*ere* Verbs

The following are some of the most common irregular –*ere* verbs:

bere – to drink
___

Gerund – *bevendo*
Past Participle – *bevuto*
Present – *bevo, bevi, beve, beviamo, bevete, bevono*
Present Subjunctive – *beva, beva, beva, beviamo, beviate, bevano*
Imperfect – *bevevo, bevevi, beveva, bevevamo, bevevate, bevevano*
Imperfect Subjunctive – *bevessi, bevessi, bevesse, bevessimo, beveste, bevessero*
Preterite – *bevvi, bevesti, bevve, bevemmo, beveste, bevvero*
Future – *berrò, berrai, berrà, berremo, berrete, berranno*
Conditional – *berrei, berresti, berrebbe, berremmo, berreste, berrebbero*
Imperative – *bevi, beva, beviamo, bevete, bevano*

cadere – to fall
___

Preterite – *caddi, cadesti, cadde, cademmo, cadeste, caddero*
Future – *cadrò, cadrai, cadrà, cadremo, cadrete, cadranno*
Conditional – *cadrei, cadresti, cadrebbe, cadremmo, cadreste, cadrebbero*

dovere – to have to, must
___

Present – *devo, devi, deve, dobbiamo, dovete, devono*
Present Subjunctive – *deva, deva, deva, dobbiamo, dobbiate (debbano), devano*
Future – *dovrò, dovrai, dovrà, dovremo, dovrete, dovranno*
Conditional – *dovrei, dovresti, dovrebbe, dovremmo, dovreste, dovrebbero*

31

potere – to be able to

Present – *posso, puoi, può, possiamo, potete, possono*
Present Subjunctive – *possa, possa, possa, possiamo, possiate, possano*
Future – *potrò, potrai, potrà, potremmo, potrete, potranno*
Conditional – *potrei, potresti, potrebbe, potremmo, potreste, potrebbero*

rimanere – to remain

Past Participle – *rimasto*
Present – *rimango, rimani, rimane, rimaniamo, rimanete, rimangano*
Present Subjunctive – *rimanga, rimanga, rimanga, rimaniamo, rimaniate, rimangano*
Preterite – *rimasi, rimanesti, rimase, rimanemmo, rimaneste, rimasero*
Future – *rimarrò, rimarrai, rimarrà, rimarremo, rimarrete, rimarrano*
Conditional – *rimarrei, rimarresti, rimarrebbe, rimarremmo, rimarreste, rimarrebbero*
Imperative – *rimani, rimanga, rimaniamo, rimanete, rimangano*

sapere – to know

Present – *so, sai, sa, sappiamo, sapete, sanno*
Present Subjunctive – *sappia, sappia, sappia, sappiamo, sappiate, sappiano*
Preterite – *seppi, sapesti, seppe, sapemmo, sapeste, seppero*
Future – *saprò, saprai, saprà, sapremo, saprete, sapranno*
Conditional – *saprei, sapresti, sprebbe, sapremmo, sapreste, saprebbero*
Imperative – *sappi, sappia, sappiamo, sappiate, sappiano*

tenere – to hold, to keep

Present – *tengo, tieni, tiene, teniamo, tenete, tengono*
Present Subjunctive – *tenga, tenga, tenga, teniamo, teniate, tengano*

Preterite – *tenni, tenesti, tenne, tenemmo, teneste, tennero*
Future – *terrò, terrai, terrà, terremo, terrete, terranno*
Conditional – *terrei, terresti, terrebbe, terremmo, terreste, terrebbero*
Imperative – *tieni, tenga, teniamo, tenete, tengano*

volere – to want

Present – *voglio, vuoi, vuole, vogliamo, volete, vogliono*
Present Subjunctive – *voglia, voglia, voglia, vogliamo, vogliate, vogliano*
Preterite – *volli, volesti, volle, volemmo, voleste, vollero*
Future – *vorrò, vorrai, vorrà, vorremo, vorrete, vorranno*
Conditional – *vorrei, vorresti, vorrebbe, vorremmo, vorreste, vorrebbero*
Imperative – *vogli, voglia, vogliamo, vogliate, vogliano*

4.3 Common Irregular –*ire* Verbs

The following are the most common irregular –*ire* verbs:

dire – to say, to tell

Gerund – *dicendo*
Past Participle – *detto*
Present – *dico, dici, dice, diciamo, dite, dicono*
Present Subjunctive – *dica, dica, dica, diciamo, diciate, dicano*
Imperfect – *dicevo, dicevi, diceva, dicevamo, dicevate, dicevano*
Imperfect Subjunctive – *dicessi, dicessi, dicesse, dicessimo, diceste, dicessero*
Preterite – *dissi, dicesti, disse, dicemmo, diceste, dissero*
Imperative – *dì, dica, diciamo, dite, dicano*

salire – to climb, to go up

Present – *salgo, sali, sale, saliamo, salite, salgono*
Present Subjunctive – *salga, salga, salga, saliamo, saliate, salgano*
Imperative – *sali, salga, saliamo, salite, salgano*

33

uscire – to go out

Present – *esco, esci, esce, usciamo, uscite, escono*
Present Subjunctive – *esca, esca, esca, usciamo, usciate, escano*
Imperative – *esci, esca, usciamo, uscite, escano*

venire – to come

Past Participle – *venuto*
Present – *vengo, vieni, viene, veniamo, venite, vengono*
Present Subjunctive – *venga, venga, venga, veniamo, veniate, vengano*
Preterite – *venni, venisti, venne, venimmo, veniste, vennero*
Future – *verrò, verrai, verrà, verremo, verrete, verranno*
Conditional – *verrei, verresti, verrebbe, verremmo, verreste, verrebbero*
Imperative – *vieni, venga, veniamo, venite, vengano*

4.4 Irregular Past Participles with *Avere*

1.	*aggiungere*	*aggiunto*	added
2.	*aprire*	*aperto*	opened
3.	*assistere*	*assistito*	assisted
4.	*assumere*	*assunto*	assumed
5.	*chiedere*	*chiesto*	asked
6.	*chiudere*	*chiuso*	closed
7.	*cogliere*	*colto*	picked
8.	*comprendere*	*compreso*	understood
9.	*concludere*	*concluso*	concluded
10.	*conoscere*	*conosciuto*	known
11.	*correggere*	*corretto*	corrected
12.	*correre*	*corso*	run
13.	*corrispondere*	*corrisposto*	corresponded
14.	*cuocere*	*cotto*	cooked
15.	*decidere*	*deciso*	decided
16.	*difendere*	*difeso*	defended
17.	*dipendere*	*dipeso*	depended
18.	*dipingere*	*dipinto*	depicted

19.	*discutere*	*discusso*	discussed
20.	*dividere*	*diviso*	divided
21.	*esprimere*	*espresso*	expressed
22.	*fingere*	*finto*	feigned
23.	*immergere*	*immerso*	immersed
24.	*leggere*	*letto*	read
25.	*mettere*	*messo*	placed
26.	*mordere*	*morso*	bitten
27.	*muovere*	*mosso*	moved
28.	*nascondere*	*nascosto*	hidden
29.	*offendere*	*offeso*	offended
30.	*parere*	*parso*	seemed
31.	*perdere*	*perso/perduto*	lost
32.	*persuadere*	*persuaso*	persuaded
33.	*piangere*	*pianto*	cried
34.	*piovere*	*piovuto*	rained
35.	*prendere*	*preso*	taken
36.	*promettere*	*promesso*	promised
37.	*raccogliere*	*raccolto*	collected
38.	*ridere*	*riso*	laughed
39.	*risolvere*	*risolto*	resolved
40.	*rispondere*	*risposto*	answered
41.	*rompere*	*rotto*	broken
42.	*sapere*	*saputo*	known
43.	*scegliere*	*scelto*	chosen
44.	*scoprire*	*scoperto*	discovered
45.	*scrivere*	*scritto*	written
46.	*soffrire*	*sofferto*	suffered
47.	*sorridere*	*sorriso*	smiled
48.	*spegnere*	*spento*	extinguished, turned off
49.	*spendere*	*speso*	spent
50.	*togliere*	*tolto*	taken
51.	*uccidere*	*ucciso*	killed
52.	*vedere*	*visto*	seen
53.	*vincere*	*vinto*	won, conquered

4.5 Irregular Past Participles with *Essere*

1. *crescere*	*cresciuto*	grown
2. *discendere*	*disceso*	descended
3. *essere*	*stato*	been
4. *morire*	*morto*	died
5. *nascere*	*nato*	born
6. *piacere*	*piacuto*	pleased
7. *rimanere*	*rimasto*	remained
8. *scendere*	*sceso*	come down
9. *venire*	*venuto*	came

4.6 Irregular Present Gerunds

Most verbs with irregular present gerunds are formed from the stem of the *–io* present tense.

Present Indicative	Verb	Present Gerund
fare	*io faccio*	*facendo*
dire	*io dico*	*dicendo*

CHAPTER 5

Numbers and Time

5.1 Cardinal Numbers

0	zero	11	undici	22	ventidue
1	uno	12	dodici	23	ventitrè
2	due	13	tredici	28	ventotto*
3	tre	14	quattordici	30	trenta
4	quattro	15	quindici	40	quaranta
5	cinque	16	sedici	50	cinquanta
6	sei	17	diciassette	60	sessanta
7	sette	18	diciotto	70	settanta
8	otto	19	diciannove	80	ottanta
9	nove	20	venti	90	novanta
10	dieci	21	ventuno*	100	cento

200	duecento	900	novecento
300	trecento	1000	mille
400	quattrocento	1001	mille(e) uno
500	cinquecento	2000	duemila
600	seicento	1,000,000	un milione
700	settecento	2,000,000	due milioni
800	ottocento	1,000,000,000	un miliardo

* Note: 21, 28, 31, 38, etc. drop the last vowel before adding *uno* and *otto*. For 23, 33, etc. add an accent on the *è*.

The nouns *milione* and *miliardo* and their plurals (*milioni*, *miliardi*) require the preposition *di* before another noun.

due milioni di dollari – two million dollars

All of the cardinal numbers except *uno* and *mille* are invariable in form. Cardinal numbers usually precede nouns.
Un is never used before *cento* or *mille*. For example,

cento macchine – 100 cars
mille studenti – 1000 students

5.1.1 Special Use when Referring to Centuries

Italian uses the following forms when referring to centuries:

il secolo tredicesimo – *il Duecento* – the 13th century
il secolo quattordicesimo – *il Trecento* – the 14th century
il secolo quindicesimo – *il Quattrocento* – the 15th century
il secolo sedicesimo – *il Cinquecento* – the 16th century
il secolo diciassettesimo – *il Seicento* – the 17th century
il secolo diciottesimo – *il Settecento* – the 18th century
il secolo diciannovesimo – *l' Ottocento* – the 19th century
il secolo ventesimo – *il Novecento* – the 20th century

5.2   Ordinal Numbers

Ordinal numbers are adjectives. They agree in gender and in number with the nouns they precede.

la sesta studentessa – the sixth student
i primi due giorni – the first two days

1st	primo(a/i/e)	11th	undicesimo(a/i/e)
2nd	secondo(a/i/e)	12th	dodicesimo(a/i/e)
3rd	terzo(a/i/e)	13th	tredicesimo(a/i/e)
4th	quarto(a/i/e)	14th	quattordicesimo(a/i/e)
5th	quinto(a/i/e)	15th	quindicesimo(a/i/e)
6th	sesto(a/i/e)	16th	sedicesimo(a/i/e)
7th	settimo(a/i/e)	17th	diciassettesimo(a/i/e)
8th	ottavo(a/i/e)	18th	diciottesimo(a/i/e)
9th	nono(a/i/e)	19th	diciannovesimo(a/i/e)
10th	decimo(a/i/e)	20th	ventesimo(a/i/e)

To form ordinal numbers after *undici* add *–esimo* to the cardinal number: *l'undicesimo.*

5.3 Expressing Time

Che ora è? is used in the singular.
Che ore sono? is used for plural.

del mattino (A.M.)
del pomeriggio (P.M.)
di sera (P.M.)

È mezzogiorno (P.M.)
È mezzanotte (A.M.)

Time at the hour
A che ora è la prima colazione?...la colazione?...la cena? At what time is breakfast?...lunch?...supper?

È alle otto. È a mezzogiorno. È alle sei. It is at eight o'clock. It is at 12:00 noon. It is at six o'clock.
All'una. At one o'clock.

Note: Airports, train stations, and T.V. programs, as well as all official timetables, use a 24 hour clock.

sono le tredici = 13:00 = 1:00 P.M.
sono le diciotto e trenta = 18:30 = 6:30 P.M.

CHAPTER 6

Days, Months, Seasons, and Dates

6.1 Days of the Week

Quali sono i giorni della settimana? What are the days of the week?

I giorni della settimana sono: The days of the week are:

lunedì	Monday
martedì	Tuesday
mercoledì	Wednesday
giovedì	Thursday
venerdì	Friday
sabato	Saturday
domenica	Sunday

6.2 Months of the Year

Quali sono i mesi dell'anno? What are the months of the year?

I mesi dell'anno sono: The months of the year are:

gennaio	January
febbraio	February

41

marzo	March
aprile	April
maggio	May
giugno	June
luglio	July
agosto	August
settembre	September
ottobre	October
novembre	November
dicembre	December

Note: The days of the week and the months of the year are not capitalized.

The word *on* is not expressed before the names of days.

Sono andato al teatro sabato. I went to the theater on Saturday.
Vado al teatro il sabato. I go to the theater on Saturdays (meaning every Saturday).

In Italian the word *on* is expressed by the definite article before the date.

Antonio è nato il 9 gennaio 1994. Anthony was born on January 9, 1994.
Il primo gennaio. On January 1st.

The word *in* is expressed by the preposition *in* or *a* before the names of months, depending on individual style.

Anna è nata in luglio. Anne was born in July.

6.3 Seasons and Weather

Le stagioni dell'anno sono: The seasons of the year are:

la primavera	spring
l'estate	summer

l'autunno	autumn
l'inverno	winter

To express something which takes place during a season, use the preposition *in* or *di.*

in primavera – in spring
in estate – in summer
in autunno – in autumn
in inverno – in winter

6.3.1 Idioms

Fa freddo d'inverno. It is cold in winter.

Che tempo fa? How is the weather?

Fa freddo. It is cold.
Fa caldo. It is warm (It is hot).
Fa fresco. It is cool.
C'è il sole. It is sunny.
È nuvoloso. It is cloudy.
Tira vento. It is windy.
Fa buon tempo. It is good weather.
Fa bel tempo. It is nice weather.
Fa mal tempo. It is bad weather.
Fa brutto tempo. It is bad weather.
Piove. It is raining.
Nevica. It is snowing.
C'è la nebbia. It is foggy.

In primavera piove molto. It rains a lot in the spring.
In inverno nevica. It snows in the winter.
In autunno tira vento. It is windy in autumn.
In estate fa molto caldo. It is very hot in the summer.

6.4 Dates

Che giorno è? What day is it?
Qual'è la data di oggi? What is today's date?

To express a date, reverse the order of the day and the month and use the definite article *il* with the cardinal number.

Note: To express the first of the month use the ordinal number *primo*.

Oggi è il primo gennaio 1994. Today is January 1st, 1994.
Oggi è il 14 agosto 1982. Today is August 14th, 1982.

CHAPTER 7

Topical Vocabulary

7.1 Home

la casa – home
l'appartamento – apartment
la camera da letto – bedroom
la stanza da bagno – bathroom
il salotto – living room
il giardino – garden
il garage – garage
la tavola – table
la poltrona – armchair
il frigorifero – refrigerator
la lampada – lamp
lo specchio – mirror

la casa – house
la sala da pranzo – dining room
la cucina – kitchen
l'ascensore – elevator
le scale – stairs
i mobili – furnishings
la sedia – chair
il divano – sofa
il letto – bed
il tappeto – rug
il televisore – television

7.2 Foods

i cibi – foods
il pane – bread
la carne – meat
la minestra – broth
il burro – butter
il gelato – ice cream

il formaggio – cheese
il pesce – fish
l'uovo, le uova – egg, eggs
la torta – cake

7.3 Beverages

le bevande – beverages
il vino – wine
l'acqua – water
il tè – tea
il caffè – coffee
il succo d'arancia – orange juice

la birra – beer
l'acqua minerale – mineral water
il latte – milk
l'aranciata – orange soda

7.4 Vegetables

vegetali/legumi – vegetables/legumes
la verdura/gli ortaggi – vegetables
i fagiolini – string beans
i broccoli – broccoli
il sedano – celery
l'insalata – salad
l'aglio – garlic

le patate – potatoes
i piselli – peas
le carote – carrots
i peperoni – peppers
le cipolle – onions
i pomodori – tomatoes

7.5 Recreation

la ricreazione/gli svaghi – recreation/leisure
il video registratore – VCR
il giradischi – record player

il concerto – concert
il ballo – dance

il registratore – tape recorder
i giochi informatici – computer games
la musica – music
il cinema – movies

7.6 Sports

gli sport – sports
il calcio – soccer

il tennis – tennis
il bowling – bowling
sciare/lo sci – to ski/skiing
il karatè – karate

la palla a canestro/il basket – basketball
il golf – golf
il nuoto – swimming
la palla a volo – volleyball
fare l'aerobica – aerobics

7.7 Parts of the Body

le parti del corpo – parts of the body

la faccia/il viso – face	*l'occhio/gli occhi* – eye/eyes
il naso – nose	*la mano/le mani* – hand/hands
la bocca – mouth	*la lingua* – tongue
il dente/i denti – tooth/teeth	*il petto* – chest
il cuore – heart	*la gamba/le gambe* – leg/legs
il dito/le dita – finger/fingers	*il piede/i piedi* – foot/feet
il braccio/le braccia – arm/arms	*il ginocchio/i ginocchi* – knee/knees

7.8 Colors

i colori – colors

rosso – red	*giallo* – yellow
nero – black	*bianco* – white
azzurro – blue	*celeste* – light blue
marrone – brown	*arancione* – orange
verde – green	*rosa* – pink
grigio – gray	*viola* – violet
blu – blue	*lilla* – lilac

7.9 Clothing

il vestiario – clothing

il cappotto – coat	*il vestito/l'abito* – suit/dress
i pantaloni – pants	*la cravatta* – tie
la camicia – shirt	*il cappello* – hat
la veste – dress	*la gonna* – skirt
la scarpa/le scarpe – shoe/shoes	*i calzini* – socks
l'impermeabile – raincoat	

7.10 Jewelry

i gioelli – jewelry

l'orologio – watch	*il bracciale* – bracelet
gli orecchini – earrings	*l'anello* – ring
la collana – necklace	*la spilla* – pin

7.11 Occupations

i mestieri – occupations
l'avvocato – lawyer
il farmacista – pharmacist
l'infermiera – nurse
il banchiere – banker
il professore – professor
il programmatore d'informatica –
    computer programmer

il medico – doctor
l'ingegnere – engineer
il giornalista – journalist
il poliziotto – policeman
l'elettricista – electrician

7.12 Transportation

trasportazione – transportation
l'aeroplano – airplane

la metropolitana – subway
il tassì – taxi
la bicicletta – bicycle
la nave – ship
il tram – street car

la macchina/l'automobile – car/
    automobile
l'autobus – bus
il piroscafo – steamship
la motocicletta – motorcycle
il treno – train

7.13 Courses

i corsi – courses
l'informatica – computer science
la chimica – chemistry
la matematica – mathematics
le scienze politiche – political
    science
la storia dell'arte – art history
l'italiano – Italian
lo spagnolo – Spanish
il giapponese – Japanese
l'inglese – English

la biologia – biology
la fisica – physics
la psicologia – psychology
la storia – history

le lingue – languages
il francese – French
il cinese – Chinese
il russo – Russian

7.14 Fruit

la frutta – fruit
la mela – apple
la banana – banana
l'uva – grapes
la ciliegia – cherry
il limone – lemon
l'arachide – peanut

la pera – pear
l'arancia – orange
il pompelmo – grapefruit
l'ananas – pineapple
il melone – melon

7.15 Animals

gli animali – animals
il cane – dog
l'uccello – bird
il leone – lion
la mucca/la vacca – cow
l'elefante – elephant
il topo – mouse
la pecora – sheep
la giraffa – giraffe

il gatto – cat
il pesce – fish
il cavallo – horse
la tigre – tiger
la scimmia – monkey
l'asino – donkey
l'agnello – lamb

CHAPTER 8

Nouns and Definite and Indefinite Articles

8.1 The Gender of Nouns

Most nouns which end in –*o* are masculine, and those which end in –*a* are feminine. Nouns which end in –*e* can be either masculine or feminine. Their gender must be memorized. For example:

il gallo – rooster
la casa – house
il professore – professor
la conversazione – conversation

Note: Most nouns ending in –*ore* are masculine, and most nouns ending in –*zione* are feminine.

Italian nouns usually form the plural as follows:

				Singular	Plural
Masculine	*o*	⇒	*i*	*il gallo*	*i galli*
Feminine	*a*	⇒	*e*	*la casa*	*le case*

Masculine or Feminine	Singular	Plural
e ⇒ i	*il professore*	*i professori*
	la conversazione	*le conversazioni*

8.2 Common Exceptions to the Rule

Most words endings in *−amma, −ema* are masculine.

Singular	Plural	
il telegramma	*i telegrammi*	telegram(s)
il programma	*i programmi*	program(s)
il problema	*i problemi*	problem(s)

Although they end in a *−o*, the following words are feminine:

Singular	Plural	
la radio	*le radi*	radio(s)
la mano	*le mani*	hand(s)
la foto	*le fote*	photo(s)

Although they end in a *−a*, the following words are masculine:

Singular	Plural	
il clima	*i climi*	climate(s)
il pigiama	*i pigiami*	pyjamas

Words ending in *−ista* are masculine or feminine depending on the gender of the person to whom it refers.

	Singular	Plural	
Masculine:	*il dentista*	*i dentisti*	dentist(s)
Feminine:	*la dentista*	*le dentiste*	
Masculine:	*il farmacista*	*i farmacisti*	pharmacist(s)
Feminine:	*la farmacista*	*le farmaciste*	

8.3 Irregular Plurals

Words ending in *–co, –ca* and *–go, –ga,* add *h* when changed to the plural.

Singular	Plural	
l'amica	*le amiche*	friend(s)
la collega	*le colleghe*	colleague(s)
il sacco	*i sacchi*	bag(s)
il dialogo	*i dialoghi*	dialogue(s)

Masculine nouns ending in *–io* drop the *o* when changed to the plural.

Singular	Plural	
l'ufficio	*gli uffici*	office(s)
lo studio	*gli studi*	study(ies)

Feminine nouns ending in *–cia* and *–gia* change to *–ce* and *–ge* when changed to the plural.

Singular	Plural	
la doccia	*le docce*	shower(s)
la pioggia	*le piogge*	rain(s)

One exception to the rule is:

la camicia	*le camicie*	shirt(s)

Masculine and feminine nouns ending in a final written accent do not change in the plural.

Singular	Plural	
la città	*le città*	city/ies
il caffè	*i caffè*	coffee(s)

Nouns ending in *–i,* like those ending in a final written accent, are invariable in the plural.

la crisi	*le crisi*	crise(s)
il tè	*i tè*	tea(s)
la gru	*le gru*	crane(s)

Nouns ending in *–ie* are invariable, the plural; for example, *la serie, le serie* (series).

Exception:
la moglie – wife   *le mogli* – wives

These words are irregular in the plural:

Singular	**Plural**	
la moglie	*le mogli*	wife/wives
l'uomo	*gli uomini*	man/men
l'uovo	*le uova*	egg(s)

Foreign nouns are usually masculine and are always written in a singular form.

il film	*i film*	film(s)
lo sport	*gli sport*	sport(s)

8.4 Suffixes

When added to a noun, the following suffixes express a diminutive, or may be used to show feelings of endearment: *–uccio, –ello, –ino, –etto*.

il cavallo – horse	*il cavaluccio* – cute little horse
l'asino – donkey	*l'asinello* – little donkey
l'uccello – bird	*l'uccellino* – little bird
il vecchio – old man	*il vecchietto* – dear old man

The suffix *–one* indicates largeness.

il libro – the book	*il librone* – the big book

la febbre – the fever	*la febbrone* – the high fever
la nebbia – the fog	*il nebione* – the dense fog

The suffixes *–accio, –astro, –ucolo* are used to convey a pejorative meaning.

il ragazzo – the boy	*il ragazzaccio* – the mean boy
il giovane – young man	*il giovanastro* – good for nothing young man
la maestra – teacher	*la maestrucola* – lousy teacher

8.5 Definite Articles

There are seven definite articles in Italian.

Definite Articles	Singular Nouns
il	Masculine nouns beginning with a consonant.
lo	Masculine nouns beginning with *z* or *s* plus a consonant.
la	Feminine nouns beginning with a consonant.
l'	Masculine or feminine nouns beginning with a vowel.

Definite Articles	Plural Nouns
i	Masculine nouns beginning with a consonant.
gli	Masculine nouns beginning with a vowel, or *z* or *s* plus a consonant.
le	Feminine nouns beginning with a consonant or vowel.

Singular	Plural
il concerto	*i concerti*
lo studio	*gli studi*
lo zio	*gli zii*

la ragazza	le ragazze
l'amica	le amiche
l'italian	gli italiani

8.6 Definite Article Contractions

The following contractions occur in Italian when a definite article preceeds the prepositions *a, da, di, in,* and *su:*

	a – to	*da* –from	*di (de)* – of	*in (ne)* – in	*su* – upon, on
il	*al*	*dal*	*del*	*nel*	*sul*
lo	*allo*	*dallo*	*dello*	*nello*	*sullo*
la	*alla*	*dalla*	*della*	*nella*	*sulla*
l'	*all'*	*dall'*	*dell'*	*nell'*	*sull'*
i	*ai*	*dai*	*dei*	*nei*	*sui*
gli	*agli*	*dagli*	*degli*	*negli*	*sugli*
le	*alle*	*dalle*	*delle*	*nelle*	*sulle*

	Singular	**Plural**
with	*con + il = col*	*con + i = coi*
for, through	*per + il = pel*	*per + i = pei*

The other definite articles do not contract with *con* and *per.*

8.7 Indefinite Articles

There are four indefinite articles in Italian:

Indefinite Article	**Singular Nouns**
un	Masculine nouns beginning with a consonant.
uno	Masculine nouns beginning with *z* or *s* plus a consonant.
una	Feminine nouns beginning with a consonant.
un'	Feminine nouns beginning with a vowel.

un concerto	*uno studio*
uno zio	*una ragazza*
un'amica	*un'aeroplano*

The plural of the indefinite article is equivalent to the partitive article (some or any). See the table for the contraction of the definite article with the preposition *di*.

Di takes the place of the partitive plus the article in expressions of quantity.

un bicchiere di birra – a glass of beer
un chilo di pesche – a kilogram of peaches
una dozzina di uova – a dozen of eggs
un litro di vino – a liter of wine
un pò di silenzio – a little of silence
una tazza di espresso – a cup of coffee

CHAPTER 9

Regular and Irregular Adjectives

9.1 Regular Adjectives

Adjectives agree in gender and number with the words they modify. Most adjectives end in –o and have four forms: masculine singular, feminine singular, masculine plural, and feminine plural.

Giovanni è americano. (–o, masculine singular)
Maria è americana. (–a, feminine singular)
I ragazzi sono americani. (–i, masculine plural)
Le ragazze sono americane. (–e, feminine plural)

These adjectives, ending in –o, usually follow the noun they modify:

allegro – happy
avaro – stingy
bravo – fine
cattivo – bad
delizioso – delicious
leggero – light
moderno – modern
pieno – full

alto – tall, high
basso – short, low
buono – good
contento – content, happy
generoso – generous
melodioso – melodious
nuovo – new
povero – poor

ricco – rich	*scontento* – unhappy
stretto – narrow	*timido* – timid
unico – only, unique	*vecchio* – old
vero – true	*vuoto* – empty

9.2 Irregular Adjectives

Adjectives ending in *–e* take an *–i* in the plural.

La signora è forte. The lady is strong.
I signori sono forti. The gentlemen are strong.

The following *–e* adjectives are common:

agile – agile, nimble	*breve* – short
celebre – famous	*debole* – weak
difficile – difficult	*eccellente* – excellent
facile – easy	*felice* – happy
grande – great, large	*importante* – important
intelligente – intelligent	*interessante* – interesting
inutile – useless, unnecessary	*triste* – sad
universale – universal	*utile* – useful
veloce – fast	

Adjectives ending in *–co, –go, –ca,* and *–ga* add an *h* before the plural ending.

Il gatto è bianco. I gatti sono bianchi. The cat is white. The cats are white.
La strada è larga. Le strade sono larghe. The street is wide. The streets are wide.

Adjectives ending in *–cio, –gio, –cia,* and *–gia* form plurals by changing to *–ci, –gi, –ce,* and *–ge,* respectively.

La pera è marcia. Le pere sono marce. The pear is rotten. The pears are rotten.

9.3 Shortened Adjectives

Some adjectives take a shortened form when placed before the noun.

Nouns beginning with a:

Masculine Singular Consonant	Feminine Singular Consonant
un bel ragazzo – a handsome boy	*una bella ragazza* – a beautiful girl
un gran maestro – a great teacher	*una gran maestra* – a great teacher
San Paolo – St. Paul	*Santa Rosa* – St. Rose
un buon libro – a good book	*una buona ragazza* – a good girl

Nouns beginning with a:

Masculine Singular Vowel	Feminine Singular Vowel
un bell'uomo – a handsome man	*una bell'amica* – a beautiful friend
un grande artista – a great artist	*una grande artista* – a great artist
Sant'Angelo – St. Angelo	*Sant'Anna* – St. Anna

Masculine Singular Nouns (beginnning with z or s plus a consonant)
   un bello zio – a handsome uncle
   Santo Stefano – St. Stephen
   un buono studente – a good student

Note: *un grand'uovo* – for words beginning in *u*.

Nouns beginning with a:

Masculine Plural Consonant	Feminine Plural Consonant
dei bei ragazzi – the handsome boys	*delle belle ragazze* – the beautiful girls
dei grandi maestri – the great teachers	*delle grandi maestre* – the great teachers

dei buoni libri – the good
books

delle buone ragazze – the good
girls

Nouns beginning with a:
Masculine Plural Vowel
dei begli uomini – the
handsome men
dei grandi artisti – the great
artisti
dei buoni amici – the good
friends

Feminine Plural Vowel
delle belle amiche – the beautiful
friends
delle grandi artisti – the great
artisti
delle buone amiche – the good
friends

9.4 Titles

Drop the *–e* in the following titles before proper names:

Signor Daidone
Dottor Lombardo
Professor Rossi

9.5 Comparison of Adjectives

The following adjectives are used in comparison:

Io mangio tanta carne quanto mia sorella. (tanto...quanto) I eat
as much meat as my sister.

Note: The *quanto* and *tanto* adjectives agree in gender and number with the nouns they modify. The adverbs *tanto* and *quanto* are invariable. Personal pronouns following *quanto* are disjunctive pronouns.

Maria è tanto alta quanto lui. Marie is as tall as he.

Cristoforo ha più soldi di Raimondo. (più di) Christopher has
more money than Raymond.

Vittoria ha meno amici di Giovanna. (meno di) Victoria has fewer
friends than Giovanna.

9.6 Relative Superlative of Adjectives

To form the superlative of an adjective, use the definite article
before *più* or *meno* and place *di* + the definite article after the adjective.

> *Roma è la più grande città dell'Italia.* Rome is the largest city in
> Italy.

> *Mario è il meno forte del gruppo.* Mario is the least strong in the
> group.

9.7 Absolute Superlative of Adjectives

To form the absolute superlative, drop the final vowel of the adjective and then add the suffix *–issimo/a/i/e*. This changes the meaning to "most" or "very."

> *La ragazza è bella. La ragazza è bellissima.* The girl is beautiful.
> The girl is very beautiful.

> *Caterina è intelligente. Caterina è intelligentissima.* Catherine
> is intelligent. Catherine is very intelligent.

9.8 Irregular Comparatives and Superlatives

The following adjectives have irregular comparative and superlative forms:

Positive	Comparative	Relative Superlative	Absolute Superlative
buono – good	*migliore* – better	*il migliore* – best	*ottimo* – very good
cattivo – bad	*peggiore* – worse	*il peggiore* – worst	*pessimo* – very bad

grande –	maggiore –	il maggiore –	massimo –
large	larger	largest	very large
piccolo –	minore –	il minore –	minimo –
small	smaller	smallest	very small

Roberto è il migliore studente di tutti. Robert is the best student of all.

Questa ragazza è la peggiore della classe. This girl is the worst in the class.

I miei fratelli sono i minori di tutta la famiglia. My brothers are the youngest of the family.

9.9 Possessive Adjectives

	Singular		Plural	
	Masculine	**Feminine**	**Masculine**	**Feminine**
my	*il mio*	*la mia*	*i miei*	*le mie*
your (familiar)	*il tuo*	*la tua*	*i tuoi*	*le tue*
you (formal)	*il Suo*	*la Sua*	*i Suoi*	*le Sue*
his, her, its	*il suo*	*la sua*	*i suoi*	*le sue*
our	*il nostro*	*la nostra*	*i nostri*	*le nostre*
your (familiar)	*il vostro*	*la vostra*	*i vostri*	*le vostre*
your (formal)	*il Loro*	*la Loro*	*i Loro*	*le Loro*
their	*il loro*	*la loro*	*i loro*	*le loro*

Il mio vestito è nero. My suit is black.
La mia macchina è bianca. My car is white.

Note: The definite article is dropped before an unmodified family relatonship in the singular.

Mia madre è bionda. My mother is blonde.
La sua futura sposa è ricca. His future wife is rich.

Exception: The definite article is retained when using *loro,* and when placed in front of *babbo, mamma, nonno,* or *nonna.*

Il mio babbo e il loro nonno sono generosi. My dad and their
grandpa are generous.

9.10 Demonstrative Adjectives

Questo (this) has four forms and agrees in gender and number
with the noun it modifies.

questo ragazzo – this boy	*questi ragazzi* – these boys
questa ragazza – this girl	*queste ragazze* – these girls

Note: Use *quest'* before nouns beginning with a vowel.

quest'anelli – these rings

Quello has the following forms:

Before a masculine singular noun beginning with a consonant:

quel
quel libro – that book

Before a feminine singular noun beginning with a consonant:

quella
quella ragazza – that girl

Before a masculine plural noun beginning with a consonant:

quei
quei libri – those books

Before a feminine plural noun beginning with a consonant:

quelle
quelle ragazze – those girls

Before a masculine or feminine singular noun beginning with a vowel:

quell'
quell'orologio – that watch
quell'amica – that friend

Before a masculine singular noun beginning with *z* or *s* plus a consonant:

quello
quello specchio – that mirror

Before a plural noun beginning with a vowel, or *z* or *s* plus a consonant:

quegli
quegli zii – those uncles

Questi libri sono difficili ma quei libri sono facili. These books are difficult, but those are easy.

CHAPTER 10

Pronouns

10.1 Subject Pronouns

Singular	Plural
io – I	*noi* – we
tu – you (familiar)	*voi* – you (familiar)
	loro – they (masculine/feminine)
lui, egli – he	*esse* – they (masculine)
lei, ella – she	*essi* – they (feminine)
Lei – you (formal)	*Loro* – you (formal)

10.2 Direct Object Pronouns

The direct object pronouns agree in gender and in number with the noun that they replace. The pronouns preceed the verb except in the imperative.

Carlo legge il libro. Carl reads the book.
Carlo lo legge. Carl reads it.

Leggete i libri. Read the books.
Leggeteli. Read them.

10.2.1 *La, Li, Le*

The direct object pronouns meaning "you" (formal) are always capitalized.

La – you (masculine/feminine singular)
Li – you (masculine plural)
Le – you (feminine plural)
L' – you (masculine/feminine singular/plural before vowels and silent *h*)

Signora Rossi, conosco Lei? Do I know you, Mrs. Rossi?
Signora Rossi, La conosco. Mrs. Rossi, I know you.

10.2.2 *Lo*

Lo as an object pronoun replaces an entire idea.

Sei sicuro che andrai in Africa l'anno prossimo? Are you certain that you will go to Africa next year?
Si' lo sono. Yes, I am certain of it.
No, non lo sono. No, I am not sure of it.

10.3 Indirect Object Pronouns *Mi, Ti, Ci,* and *Vi*

Pronoun	Direct Object	Indirect Object
mi	me	to me
ti	you	to you (informal singular)
ci	us	to us
vi	you	to you (informal plural)

Laura ci chiama. Laura calls us.
Laura ci da i soldi. Laura gives (to) us the money.

10.4 Indirect Object Pronouns *Gli, Le,* and *Loro*

gli	to him
le	to her
loro	to them

Gli and *le* precede the verb. *Loro* follows the verb.

Tu scrivi (a Giuseppe). Tu gli scrivi. You write to Joseph. You
write to him.
Tu scrivi (a Maria). Tu le scrivi. You write to Mary. You write to
her.
Tu scrivi (agli amici). Tu scrivi loro. You write to the friends.
You write to them.

Note: *Le* and *Loro* are the formal indirect object pronouns meaning "you" or "to you."

Le comes before the verb.
Loro comes after the verb.

Signor Napoli, scrivo a Lei? Mr. Napoli, am I writing to you?
Signor Napoli, Le scrivo. Mr. Napoli, am I writing to you?

10.5 *Ci*

The pronoun *ci* changes the meaning of certain verbs.

credere – to believe	*crederci* – to believe in something
mettere – to put	*metterci* – to take (time)
pensare – to think	*pensarci* – to think about it (of it)
riflettere – to reflect	*rifletterci* – to think something over
vedere – to see	*vederci* – to be able to see
volere – to want	*volerci* – to take (time, space, etc.)

Ci vogliono cento dollari per fare centosessanta mila lire. It takes
one hundred dollars to make one hundred and sixty thou-
sand lire.

10.6 *Ne*

The pronoun *ne* means "some," "any," "about," "of it," "of them,"
"from it," "from them," and "from there." *Ne* replaces a prepositional
phrase beginning with *da* or *di.*

Ho cinque fratelli. Ne ho cinque. I have five brothers. I have five of them.

Quanti ne abbiamo oggi? Ne abbiamo sei. What date is today? Today it is the 6th. (literally) How many do we have today?

10.7 Double Object Pronouns

Indirect object pronouns come before the direct object pronouns. *Mi, ti, ci,* and *vi* become *me, te, ce,* and *ve,* respectively, before the direct object pronouns.

Direct Object	Indirect Object			
	mi	*ti*	*ci*	*vi*
lo	*me lo*	*te lo*	*ce lo*	*ve lo*
la	*me la*	*te la*	*ce la*	*ve la*
l'	*me l'*	*te l'*	*ce l'*	*ve l'*
li	*me li*	*te li*	*ce li*	*ve li*
le	*me le*	*te le*	*ce le*	*ve le*
ne	*me ne*	*te ne*	*ce ne*	*ve ne*

Carmela porta il pacco a noi. Carmela brings the package to us.
Carmela ce lo porta. Carmela brings it to us.

10.8 *Glielo, Gliela, Glieli,* and *Gliele*

Direct Object	Indirect Object		
	gli (to him)	*le* (to her)	*Le* (to you, formal)
lo	*glielo*	*glielo*	*Glielo*
la	*gliela*	*gliela*	*Gliela*
l'	*gliel'*	*gliel'*	*Gliel'*
li	*glieli*	*glieli*	*Glieli*
le	*gliele*	*gliele*	*Glieli*
ne	*gliene*	*gliene*	*Gliene*

Note: Uppercase *G* indicates the formal *Le*.

Danno i libri a Cristoforo. They give the books to Christopher.
Glieli danno. They give them to him.

10.9 *Loro*

The object of pronouns *loro* (to them) and *Loro* (to you – formal plural) always follow the verb.

Danno le penne a Loro. They give the pens to you.
Le danno loro. They give them to you.

10.10 Pronouns in Informal Commands

An informal command uses the *tu, noi,* or *voi* form of the imperative.

Object pronouns are attached to the affirmative verb in informal commands. The object pronouns double the first letter when beginning with *m* or *l* if the verb is one syllable. However, in a negative command, the object pronoun precedes the verb.

Dammela! Give it to me!
Non me la dare! Don't give it to me!

10.11 Pronouns in Formal Commands

A formal command uses the *Lei* and *Loro* form of the imperative. In a formal command, the object pronouns precede an affirmative or negative command.

Me la dia! Give it to me!
Non me la dia! Don't give it to me!

10.12 Disjunctive Pronouns

Disjunctive pronouns are the same as the subject pronouns with the following exceptions: *io* becomes *me, tu* becomes *te,* and *egli* becomes *lui.* For example,

Siamo qui per lui. We are here for him.

In the present perfect tense conjugated with *avere,* the past participle agrees with the preceding direct object pronoun in gender and number. For example,

Ho dato la penna a Gianni. I gave the pen to Johnny.
L'ho data a Gianni. I gave it to Johnny.

CHAPTER 11

Adverbs

11.1 Regular Adverbs

To form an adverb from an adjective, add the suffix –*mente* to the feminine singular form of the adjective, as the following table shows:

Adjective (masculine singular)	Adjective (feminine singular)	Adverb
lento – slow	*lenta* – slow	*lentamente* – slowly
sincero – sincere	*sincera* – sincere	*sinceramente* – sincerely
triste – sad	*triste* – sad	*tristemente* – sadly

Adjectives ending in –*le* or –*re* drop the final *e* before adding –*mente*.

facile – easy   *facilmente* – easily
particolare – particular   *particolarmente* – particularly

11.2 Irregular Adverbs

The following adverbs do not end in –*mente*

adesso – now	*non* – not
allora – then	*ora* – now
anche – also	*più* – more
ancora – yet, still	*poco* – little
bene – well	*poi* – then
così – so, thus	*presto* – quickly, soon, early
dopo – later, afterwards	*qui, qua* – here
già – already	*sempre* – always
insieme – together	*spesso* – often
là, lì – there	*subito* – at once, soon, immediately
lontano – far	*tanto* – so, so much
mai – ever, never	*tardi* – late
male – badly	*troppo* – too, too much
meno – less	*vicino* – near
molto – very, much, a great deal	*volentieri* – willingly

Note: *Anche* normally precedes the word it refers to. *Anche* is elided before *io,* and it may be elided before *egli, ella,* and *essi.*

Anch'io voglio andare in Italia. I also want to go to Italy.

Giovanni anche vuole andare. Giovanni vuole andare anche. John wants to go also.

11.3 Formation of Adverbs

To form an adverb, add the suffix *–mente* to the feminine singular form of the adjective. For example,

ottima   *ottimamente*

Adjectives ending in *–le* or *–re* drop the final *e* before adding *–mente.* For example,

regolare   *regolarmente*

The absolute superlative is formed by first placing the adverbs *assai* or *molto* before the adverb:

facilmente   *assai/molto facilmente*

and then by adding *–mente* to the feminine singular form of the superlative adjective:

facile   *facilissimamente*

11.4 Position

Adverbs usually follow the verb they modify. *Sempre* (always), *ancora* (still, yet), *già* (already), and *mai* (never, ever) are placed between the auxiliary verb and the past participle.

> *Carmela non lavora regolarmente.* Carmela doesn't work regularly.

> *Carmela non ha sempre lavorato.* Carmela hasn't always worked.

11.5 Irregular Comparatives and Superlatives

The following adverbs take *se* forms:

Positive	Comparative	Absolute Superlative
bene – well	*meglio* – better	*benissimo*
male – badly	*peggio* – worse	*malissimo*
molto – a lot	*più, (di più)* – more	*moltissimo*
poco – a little	*meno, di meno* – less	*pochissimo*

Come stai? Sto malissimo. How are you? I am very bad.

Glossary

l'abitante (pl. *gli abitanti*) – inhabitant/inhabitants
l'abito – suit, outfit
l'acqua – water
l'acqua minerale – mineral water
adesso – now
l'aeroplano – airplane
aggiungere – to add
agile – agile, nimble
agli = a + gli – to the
l'aglio – garlic
l'agnello – lamb
ai = a + i – to the
al = a + il – to the
alla = a + la – to the
alle = a + le – to the
allegro (m.), *allegra* (f.) – happy
all' = a + l' – to the
allo = a + lo – to the
allora – then, so, at that time
alto (m.), *alta* (f.) – tall
l'alunno – pupil
alzare – to rise, to get up
americana (f.) – American
americano (m.) – American
l'amica (f.) – friend
le amiche (f. pl.) – friends
l'ananas – pineapple
anche – also

ancora – yet, still
andare – to go
l'anello – ring
Angelica – Angela, Angelica
Angelo – Angelo
Anna – Anne
l'anno – year
Antonio – Anthony
l'appartamento – apartment
l'arachide – peanut
l'arancia – orange
l'aranciata – orange soda
arancione – orange (color)
arrabbiarsi – to get angry
arrivare – to arrive
l'artista (f./m.) – artist
l'ascensore – elevator
l'asinello – little donkey
l'asino – donkey
assai – too much
assistere – to assist
assumere – to assume
l'autobus – bus
l'automobile (f.) – car
avaro (m.), *avara* (f.) – stingy, miser
avere – to have
avere...anni – to be...years old
avere caldo – to be hot
avere fame – to be hungry
avere freddo – to be cold
avere fretta – to be in a hurry
avere paura – to be afraid
avere ragione – to be right
avere sete – to be thirsty
avere sonno – to be sleepy
avere torto – to be wrong
l'avvocato – lawyer

azzurro – blue

il babbo – dad
il ballo – dance
la banana – banana
il banchiere – banker
basso/bassa – short, low
bel, bell', bella, – beautiful, handsome, fine
bello, bei, begli, belle, bellissimo/bellissima – very handsome,
    very beautiful
bene – well
benissimo – very well
bere – to drink
la bevanda – beverage
bianco – white
un bicchiere di birra – a glass of beer
la bicicletta – bicycle
la biologia – biology
la birra – beer
blu – blue
la bocca – mouth
la bontà – goodness, kindness
il bowling – bowling
il bracciale – bracelet
il braccio/le braccia – arm/arms
bravo/brava – fine
breve – short, brief
i broccoli – broccoli
buoni/buone – good
buono/buona – good
il burro – butter

cadere – to fall
il caffè/i caffè – coffee/coffees
il calcio – soccer
caldo – warm, hot
il calzino/i calzini – sock, socks

la camera – room
la camera da letto – bedroom
la camicia – shirt
il cane – dog
capire – to understand
il cappello – hat
il cappotto – coat, overcoat
la caramella – candy
le caramelle – candies
Carmela – Carmela
la carne – meat
la carota/le carote – carrot/carrots
la casa/le case – house/houses
Caterina – Catherine
cattivo/cattiva – bad
il cavallo – horse
il cavaluccio – cute little horse
c'è – there is
celebrare – to celebrate
celebre – famous
celeste – light blue
la cena – supper
che – that
Che ora è? – What time is it?
Che ore sono? – What time is it?
Chi? – Who?
chiamare – to call
chiaro – clear
chiedere – to ask
la chiesa – church
un chilo di pesche – a kilogram (2.25 lbs.) of peaches
la chimica – chemistry
chiudere – to close
chiunque – whoever
ci – us
ci sono – there are
ce l', ce la, – to us

ce le, ce li, – to us
ce lo, ce ne – to us
la ciliegia – cherry
il cinema – cinema, movies
il cinese – Chinese
il Cinquecento – sixteenth century
le cipolle – onions
la città/le città – city/cities
la classe – class
classico/a – classical
il clima/i climi – climate/climates
cogliere – to gather, to pick
la colazione – lunch
la collana – necklace
la collega – colleague
le colleghe – colleagues
comandare – to command, to order
com'è? – How is?
come – as
come sono? – How are?
cominciare – to start, to begin
comprendere – to understand
con – with
con gli – with the
con + i = coi – with the
con + il = col – with the
con l' – with the
con la – with the
con le – with the
con lo – with the
i concerti – concerts
il concerto – concert
concludere – to conclude
conoscere – to know
consentire – to allow, to permit
contento – satisfied, content
la conversazione/le conversazioni – conversation/conversations

i corsi – courses
correggere – to correct
correre – to run
corrispondere – to correspond
la cosa – thing
così – so, thus, (like that)
così...come – as...as
la cravatta – tie
crederci – to believe in something
credere – to believe
crescere – to grow
la crisi – the crisis
Cristoforo – Christopher
la cucina – kitchen
cuocere – to cook
il cuore – heart
curioso – curious

dagli = da + gli – from the
dai = da + i – from the
dal = da + il – from the
dall' = da + l' – from the
dalla = da + la – from the
dalle = da + le – from the
dallo = da + lo – from the
dammela – give it to me
danno – they give (verb *dare*)
dare – to give
la data – date
debole – weak
decidere – to decide
il decimo – the tenth
degli = di + gli – of the
dei = di + i – of the
del = di + il – of the
delizioso/deliziosa – delicious
deliziosi/deliziose – delicious

dell' = *di* + *l'* – of the
della= *di* + *la* – of the
delle = *di* + *le* – of the
dello = *di* + *lo* – of the
il dende/i denti – tooth, teeth
il dentista/i dentisti – dentist/dentists (m.)
la dentista/le dentiste – dentist/dentists (f.)
desiderare – to wish
dia – give (verb *dare*)
il dialogo/i dialoghi – dialogue/dialogues
il diciannovesimo – nineteenth
il diciassettesimo – seventeenth
il diciottesimo – eighteenth
difendere – to defend
difficile/difficili – difficult
dipendere – to depend
dipingere – to depict
dire – to say, to tell
discendere – to descend, to go down
discutere – to discuss
dispiacersi – to be sorry
il dito/le dita – finger/fingers
il divano – sofa
diventare – to become
divertire – to amuse
divertirsi – to amuse oneself
dividere – to divide
la doccia/le docce – shower/showers
il dodicesimo – twelfth
dolere – to be painful, to hurt
domani – tomorrow
la domenica – Sunday
dopo – afterwards, later
dopo che – after
dormire – to sleep
il dottore – doctor
Dove? – Where?

dovere – to have to, to must
dovunque – wherever
una dozzina di uova – a dozen eggs
il Duecento – thirteenth century

è – is (verb *essere*)
è impossibile... – it is impossible that...
è necessario che... – it is necessary that..
è possibile... – it is possible that...
è probabile... – it is probable that...
eccellente – excellent
egli – he
l'elefante – elephant
l'elettricista – electrician
entrare – to enter
gli esercizi – excercises
l'esercizio – excercise
esigere – to demand
esprimere – to express
esse (f.) – they
essi (m.) – they
essere – to be
essere contento – to be happy
essere di – to be from, belong to
essere sorpreso – to be surprised
essere triste – to be sad

la faccia – face
facile/facili – easy
facilmente – easily
i fagiolini – string beans
fare – to do, to make
fare bel tempo – to be nice weather
fare brutto tempo – to be bad weather
fare buon tempo – to be good weather
fare caldo – to be hot

fare freddo – to be cold
fare fresco – to be cool
fare l'aerobica – to do aerobics
il farmacista/i farmacisti (m.) – pharmacist/pharmacists
la farmacista/le farmaciste (f.) – pharmacist/pharmacists
felice – happy
il figlio/i figli – son/sons
la finestra – window
fingere – to feign
finire – to finish
la fisica – physics
il foglio – sheet of paper
il formaggio – cheese
forte/forti – strong
la foto/le fote – photo/photos
il francese – French
Francia – France
il fratello/i fratelli – brother/brothers
il frigorifero – refrigerator
fumare – to smoke

il gallo/i galli – rooster/roosters
la gamba/le gambe – leg/legs
il garage – garage
il gatto/i gatti – cat/cats
il gelato – ice cream
generoso/generosa – generous
il ghiaccio – ice
già – already
giallo – yellow
Gianni – Johnny
il giapponese – Japanese
il giardino – garden
il ginocchio/i ginocchi – knee/knees
i giochi informatici – computer games
il giornalista – journalist
il giorno/i giorni – day/days

il giovanastro – good for nothing young man
il giovane – young man
Giovanna – Joan, Joanne, Johanna, Giovanna
Giovanni – John
il giradischi – record player
la giraffa – giraffe
gli – the
gli – to him
gliel', gliela, gliele, – to him/to her
glieli, glielo, gliene – to him/to her
Gliel', Gliela, Glieli – to you (formal)
Glieli, Glielo, Gliene – to you (formal)
glorioso – glorious
la gola – throat
il golf – golf
la gondola – gondola
la gonna – skirt
gran – big
grande/grandi – big
grazie – thank you
grigio – gray
la gru/le gru – crane/cranes
il gusto – taste

ho – I have (verb *avere*)

i – the
il – the
immergere – to immerse
l'impermeabile – raincoat
importante – important
in modo che – so that
l'infermiera – nurse
l'informatica – computer science
l'ingegnere – engineer
l'inglese – English
l'insalata – salad

insieme – together
insistere – to insist
intelligente – intelligent
intelligentissimo/a – intelligent
interessante – interesting
inutile – useless
io – I
l'italiano/gli italiani – Italian/Italians

il karatè – karate

l' – the
la – the
La, L' (m./f.) – you (formal)
la, l' – it, her
là – there
il lago/i laghi – lake, lakes
la lampada – lamp
larga, larghe – wide
lasciare – to let, to leave
la lavagna – chalkboard
lavare – to wash
lavarsi – to wash oneself
lavorare – to work
il lavoro – work
le – the
Le (f. pl.) – you (formal)
Le – to you
le – to her
leggere – to read
leggero/leggera – light
Lei (uppercase) – you (formal)
lei (lowercase) – she
lentamente – slowly
lento/lenta – slow
il leone – lion
il letto – bed

Li (m. pl.) – you
li – you
lì – there
il libro/i libri – book/books
lilla – light purple, lilac
il limone – lemon
la lingua – tongue, language
le lingue – tongues, languages
un litro di vino – a liter of wine
lo – the
lo, l' – it, him
lontano – far
Loro (uppercase) – you (formal, pl.)
loro (lowercase) – they, to them
Loro – to you
lui – he
il lupo – wolf

la macchina – car
la maestra – teacher
la maestrucola – lousy teacher
mai – ever, never
male – badly
malissimo – very bad
la mamma – mom, mother
mangiare – to eat
la mano/le mani – hand/hands
marcia/marce – rotten
Maria – Marie, Maria
marrone – brown
massimo – greatest
la matematica – mathematics
il mattino – morning
il medico – doctor
meglio – better
il meglio – the best
me l', me la, me le – it to me

me li, me lo, me ne – it to me
la mela – apple
melodioso/melodiosa – melodious
melone – melon
meno – less
a meno che – unless
di meno – less
il meno – the least
meno...di – fewer...than
il mese/i mesi – month/months
la metropolitana – subway
metterci – to take (time)
mettere – to put, to place
la mezzanotte – midnight
mezzo/mezza – half
il mezzogiorno – noon
mi – me
Michele – Michael
i miei, le mie – my, mine
migliore – better
il, la migliore – the best
la minestra – soup
minimo – least
minore – younger
il minore – youngest
il mio, la mia – my, mine
i mobili – furniture
moderno/moderna – modern
la moglie, le mogli – wife, wives
moltissimo – very much
molto – very, much, a great deal
mordere – to bite
morire – to die
la motocicletta – motorcycle
la mucca – cow
muovere – to move
la musica – music

nascere – to be born
nascondere – to hide
il naso – nose
la nave – ship
ne – some, any, about it, of it, of them, from it, from them, from
    there
la nebbia – fog
nebbioso – foggy
negare – to deny
negli = in + gli – in the
nei = in + i – in the
nel = in + il – in the
nell' = in + l' – in the
nella = in + la – in the
nello = in + lo – in the
nelle = in + le – in the
nero – black
nevica – it is snowing
noi – we
a noi – to us
non – not
non...affatto – not...at all
non...ancora – not...yet
non appena che – as soon as
non...che – only
non...mai – not...ever, never
non...nè...nè – neither...nor
non...neanche/nemmeno – not even
non...nessuno – nobody, not...anybody, not anyone
non...niente/nulla – nothing, not...anything
non...più – no longer, not...more
la nonna – grandmother
il nonno – grandfather
il nono – ninth
il Novecento – twentieth century
nucleare – nuclear

il nuoto – swimming
nuovo/nuova – new
nuvoloso – cloudy

l'occhio/gli occhi – eye/eyes
occorrere – to be necessary
offendere – to offend
oggi – today
ora – now
ordinare – to order, to command
gli orecchini – earrings
l'orologio – watch, clock
gli ortaggi – vegetables
l'ottavo – eighth
ottimo – very good
otto – eight
l'Ottocento – nineteenth century

il pacco – package
la palla a canestro – basketball
(il basket) – basketball
la palla a volo – volleyball
il pane – bread
il panino/i panini – roll (of bread)/rolls, sandwich/sandwiches
il pantalone – pants
Paolo – Paul
il papa – Pope
la pappa – mush, baby food
parere – to seem
parlando – speaking
parlare – to speak
particolare – particular
particolarmente – particularly
partire – to depart
la pasta – pasta
le patate – potatoes
la pecora – sheep
peggio – worse

il peggio – the worst
peggiore – worse
il peggiore – the worst
la penna/le penne – pen/pens
pensarci – to think about it (of it)
i peperoni – peppers
per – for, by, in order to, because of
pel = per + il – for the
per i = per + i – for the
per la, per le, per l' – for the
per lo, per gli – for the
la pera/le pere – pear/pears
perchè?/perchè – why?, because
perdere – to lose
permettere – to allow, to permit
persuadere – to persuade
il pesce – fish
pessimo – very bad
il petto – chest
piacere – to please
per piacere – please
piangere – to cry
il piccolo – the little boy
piccolo – little, small
il piede/i piedi – foot/feet
pieno/piena – full
il pigiama/i pigiami – pajamas
la pioggia/le piogge – rain/rains
piove – it is raining
piovere – to rain
il piroscafo – steamship
i piselli – peas
più – more, plus
più...di – more...than
di più – more
il più – the most
la pizza – pizza

un pò di silenzio – a little bit of silence
poco – a little
pochissimo – very little
poi – then
poichè – since
il poliziotto – policeman
la poltrona – armchair
il pomeriggio – afternoon
i pomodori – tomatoes
il pompelmo – grapefruit
portare – to bring
potere – to be able to, to must
povero/povera – poor
preferire – to prefer
presto – quickly, soon, early
pretendere – to demand
la prima colazione – breakfast
prima che – before
prima di – before
il primo – first
probabile – probable
il problema/i problemi – problem/problems
il professore/i professori – professor/professors, teacher/teachers
il programma/i programmi – program/programs
il programmatore d'informatica – computer programmer
proibire – to forbid
promettere – to promise
prossimo/prossima – next
la psicologia – psychology
purchè – provided that

qua – here
il quadro – picture
Quale?/Quali? – What?
qualunque – whatever
quando – when
Quanto(a,i,e)? – How much? How many?

quantunque – although
il quarto – fourth
un quarto – a quarter
il Quattrocento – fifteenth century
quei, quegli, quelle – those
quel, quello, qell' – that
quella – that
questi/queste – these
questo/questa – this
qui – here
il quindicesimo – fifteenth
il quinto – fifth

raccogliere – to collect
la radio/le radi – radio/radios
la ragazza/le ragazze – girl/girls
il ragazzaccio – mean boy
Raimondo – Raymond
il registratore – tape recorder
regolarmente – regularly
ricco/ricca – rich
richiedere – to require, to demand
ridere – to laugh
rifletterci – to think something over
rimanere – to remain
risolvere – to resolve
rispondere – to answer
ritornare – to return
Roma – Rome
rompere – to break
la rosa – rose
Rosa – Rose
rosso/rossa – red
il russo – Russian

il sacco/i sacchi – bag, bags
la sala da pranzo – dining room

salire – to go up
sapere – to know (how)
lo sbaglio – mistake
le scale – stairs
scappare – to run away
la scarpa/le scarpe – shoe/shoes
scegliere – to choose
scendere – to go down
scheletro – skeleton
schiavo – slave
lo sci – skiing
sciare – to ski
le scienze politiche – political science
la scimmia – monkey
scontento/scontenta – unhappy
scoprire – to discover
scrivere – to write
la scuola – school
se – if
sebbene – although
il secolo – century
il secondo – second
il sedano – celery
la sedia – chair
il sedicesimo – sixteenth
seicento – six hundred
il Seicento – seventeenth century
sembrare – to appear
sempre – always
senza – without
senza che – without
la sera – evening
il sesto – sixth
sete – thirsty
sette – seven
settecento – seven hundred
il Settecento – eighteenth century

la settimana – week
il settimo – seventh
si dubita che... – it is doubtful that
sicuro/sicura – safe, sure
il signore – Mr., sir, gentleman
simpatico/simpatica – nice, lovely, kind
sincera/sincero – sincere
sinceramente – sincerely
il sogno – dream
i soldi – money
il sole – sun
la sorella – sister
sorridere – to smile
gli spaghetti – spaghetti
lo spagnolo – Spanish
lo specchio – mirror
spegnere – to extinguish, to turn out
spendere – to spend
sperare – to hope
spesso – often
la spilla – pin
gli sposi – newlyweds
lo sposo – bridegroom
la stagione/le stagioni – season, seasons
la stanza da bagno – bathroom
stare – to stay (to be with health and location)
Stefano – Stephen
la storia – history
la storia dell'arte – art history
strano/strana – strange
stretto/stretta – narrow
lo studente/gli studenti – student/students
studiare – to study
lo studio/gli studi – study/studies
su – on, upon, up, over, above
subito – at once, soon, immediately
il succo d'arancia – orange juice

suggerire – to suggest
sugli = su + gli – on the
sui = su + i – on the
sul = su + il – on the
sull' = su + l' – on the
sulla = su + la – on the
sulle = su + le – on the
sullo = su + lo – on the
gli svaghi – recreations

tanta/tanto – so much
tanta...quanto – as much...as
tappeto – rug
tardi – late
il tassì – taxi
la tavola – table
una tazza di espresso – a cup of espresso
il tè/i tè – tea/teas
il tedesco – German
il telegramma/i telegrammi – telegram/telegrams
il televisore – television
temere – to fear
tempo – time
tenere – to hold
il tennis – tennis
il terzo – third
la testa – head
te l', te la, te le – it to you
te li, te lo, te ne – it to you
ti – you
la tigre – tiger
timido/timida – timid
tira vento – it is windy
tirare – to pull
toccare – to touch
togliere – to take
il topo – mouse

tornare – to return
la torta – cake
il tram – street car
la trasportazione – transportation
il Trecento – fourteenth century
il tredicesimo – thirteenth
il treno – train
triste – sad
tristemente – sadly
troppo – too much
tu – you (friendly)
tutto/tutti – all/everyone

l'uccello – bird
l'uccellino – little bird
uccidere – to kill
l'ufficio/gli uffici – office/offices
un, un', una, uno – a, an
l'undicesimo – eleventh
undici – eleven
unico/unica – unique
universale – universal
uno – one
l'uomo/gli uomini – man, men
l'uovo/le uova – egg, eggs
usare – to use
usato – used
uscire – to go out
utile – useful
l'uva – grape

la vacca – cow
ve l', ve la, ve le – it, to you
ve li, ve lo, ve ne – it, to you
il vecchietto – dear old man
vecchio/vecchia – old
il vecchio – old man

vederci – to be able to see
vedere – to see
veloce – fast
il ventesimo – twentieth
vendere – to sell
venire – to come
la verdura – greens, vegetables
vero, vera – true
la veste – dress
il vestiario – clothing
il vestito – suit
vi – you
vicino – near
il video registratore – V.C.R.
vietato – forbidden
vincere – to conquer, to win
il vino – wine
viola – violet, purple
visitare – to visit
il viso – face
Vittoria – Victoria
voi – you (friendly, pl.)
volentieri – willingly
volerci – to take (time, space)
volere – to wish, to want
vuoto – empty

lo zero – zero
lo zio, gli zii – uncle, uncles
lo zucchero – sugar